Grandad on the moon

In memory of Mark Lockwood,

for Leon and Luna.

Emma Louise Publishing

My grandad is so special. He doesn't live on earth anymore, he's on the moon in outer space.

He has so many fun adventures up there, he never stays in one place.

When I looked up today, he was driving a huge orange monster truck.

He raced it over the moon's craters so fast that he got the whole thing stuck.

Yesterday, up in the sky, my little sister saw him riding a graceful unicorn named Polly.

She had bright, colourful fur and a face that was always jolly.

One day, he was playing with the naughty dinosaurs. My grandad is so brave.

On Sundays, he loves to mow the long green grass in the garden of fairies.

Purple flowers cover the ground, and the trees are full of yellow canaries.

Nothing compares to when he goes fishing for sharks in the deep blue sea.

The sharks are so greedy; they consumed everything, even drunk my grandad's black tea.

I love observing the countless adventures he has. I just wish he could come back to play.

How many aliens did you find along the way?

www.ingramcontent.com/pod-product-compliance
Lightning Source LLC
Chambersburg PA
CBHW042252100526
44587CB00002B/112